THE OF
RUI
TENNIS

FOREWORD BY TIM HENMAN

INTRODUCTION BY JOHN BARRETT

Bodleian Library
UNIVERSITY OF OXFORD

Final endpapers show Battledore and Shuttlecock, a game popular in the mid-1850s.

First published in 2010 by the Bodleian Library
Broad Street, Oxford OX1 3BG

2nd impression. Reprinted in 2016

www.bodleianshop.co.uk

ISBN: 978 1 85124 318 1

Foreword © Tim Henman, 2010
Introduction and this edition © Bodleian Library, University of Oxford, 2010

Images pp. 4, 16, 17, 33, 35 © Bodleian Library, University of Oxford, 2010;
tennis court diagrams on pp. 14, 21, 52, 58, 59, 60, 61, taken, with permission, from *The Tennis Players: From Pagan Rites to Strawberries and Cream* by Tom Todd (1979). All other images © AELTC/Museum.
Every effort has been made to trace the copyright of all the pictures. If there are unintentional omissions, please contact the publisher in writing, who will correct all subsequent editions.

Cover design by Dot Little
Typeset in stone serif by JCS Publishing Services Ltd, www.jcs-publishing.co.uk
Printed and bound in Croatia by Zrinski D.D. on 80 gsm Munken Premium Bookwove Vol.17.5 sourced from an FSC accedited mill

Mixed Sources
Product group from well-managed forests, controlled sources and recycled wood or fiber
www.fsc.org Cert no. TT-COC-002303
© 1996 Forest Stewardship Council

The FSC logo identifies products that contain wood from well-managed forests, certified in accordance with the strict environmental, social and economic standards of the Forest Stewardship Council

A CIP record of this publication is available from the British Library

CONTENTS

Foreword...5

Introduction...7

The Major's Game of Lawn Tennis, in 1874 45

Rules of Lawn-Tennis, Adopted by the M.C.C.
    and the A.E.C. & L.T.C., 1878 53

Appendix: Court Plans and Dimensions..............58

FOREWORD

FROM THE START, TENNIS has been in my blood. It is part of our family history that my great-grandmother was the first woman to serve over-arm at Wimbledon and her daughter, my grandmother, was the last to serve under-arm there.

I don't think either of them would have believed how fast the players of today can serve a tennis ball. That is inevitable, I suppose, given the new training techniques. It has certainly meant that the service has a dominating effect in the modern game, especially on fast surfaces.

It was fascinating to discover in John Barrett's Introduction that in the early years of the game, 'The service line was twice moved closer to the net. In 1878, the distance was reduced from 26 to 22 feet and two years later to 21 feet, a measurement which still stands.' With several of today's leading male players standing well over 6 foot 5 inches and the average height in both the men's and women's game going up all the time, I wonder if it will ever be moved even closer. After all, a lot has changed since the days of the wooden racket.

When I was growing up at home in Oxfordshire, learning the game from my parents, my two brothers and my two uncles, all of whom were decent players, I quickly discovered that you had to spend many hours practising all aspects of the game if you wanted to win; and I did. Then, when I started to play matches in junior tournaments without umpires, I realised that you also had to know the rules backwards. It was all a steep learning curve.

Reading through the Introduction it is amazing to discover how our great sport has evolved from a simple pastime played on the back lawns of family homes and small clubs into the major multi-million-pound industry it is today. Without a sound set of rules, amended by the International Tennis Federation from time to time and applied universally, that would not have happened.

As an Oxford man, born and bred, it gives me great pleasure to be associated with this publication of the Bodleian Library. It is also appropriate that they have had the co-operation of the All England Lawn Tennis Club, for that is where I enjoyed some of my happiest tennis moments – as well as a few painful ones. I wish this excellent book every success.

TIM HENMAN

INTRODUCTION

An obscure Englishman and a rather more famous American were the catalysts for the arrival of Lawn Tennis in the second half of the nineteenth century. Yet Edwin Budding and Charles Goodyear were blissfully unaware of the part they would play in allowing the ancient game of Real Tennis or Royal Tennis (Court Tennis in the United States) to emerge from the confines of royal palaces, religious houses and a few select clubs to become a popular outdoor sport. Nor could they possibly have guessed that, over the next few years, the new game would spread throughout the world with the pace of a fierce forest fire.

Edwin Budding, an engineer from Thrupp in Gloucestershire, had patented his lawn mower in 1830. A machine with curved rotating blades, driven by the two side wheels that in turn drove gears to spin the blades, the new mower cut lawns much shorter than was possible with a sickle or scythe. Budding's original idea was developed by Alexander Shanks of Arbroath, who, in the early 1850s, produced a mower that would also roll the grass and collect the cuttings. It was the commercial success of Shanks and another producer of lawn mowers—Thomas Green of Leeds, who introduced a chain drive—that transformed the back gardens of England.

Meanwhile, across the Atlantic, Charles Goodyear was nearing the end of his long and costly quest: for twelve years he had been trying to stabilize natural rubber to produce tubing, footwear, and clothing. Eventually, in 1839, Goodyear discovered that he could produce a stable material by heating raw rubber that had been mixed with sulphur. Yet he struggled to find backers; he had let them down so often in the past with his latest method. Not until 1844, supported now by his wealthy brother-in-law, could he raise the funds to patent his process of vulcanization. It was an invention whose development would reach into the furthest corners of human activity, including sport.

At last it would be possible to produce rubber balls of varying size and height of bounce suitable for use on a grass surface that had been cut short and well rolled. The liveliness could be controlled both by the quantity and type of filler that was introduced into the rubber mix and also by the internal air pressure decided upon. These developments were fundamental to the success of Lawn Tennis.

The Evolution of Ball Games

Simple games involving balls had been played for centuries. Drawings on Egyptian tombs show ball games were in vogue in 1500 BC. In Italy and France in the fourteenth century, ball games became more organized and were played both indoors and outdoors on specially prepared open spaces and in royal palaces, castle moats, or the cloisters of monasteries and other religious buildings.

At first the ball was hit with the hand. *Jeu de Paume* was played using balls stuffed with hemp, wool, or horse-hair and covered in hand-stitched sheepskin. In an outdoor version of the game, called *Jeu de Longue Paume*, the players began to wear gloves and used rackets with parchment stretched across the face, the *battoir* (right), to hit balls covered in stitched cloth. In his *Annals of Tennis*, published in 1878, Julian Marshall describes how the gut strung racket replaced the *battoir* because not only could cat gut be 'more plentifully procured than vellum or parchment, but on account of the greater effect on the ball which could be produced by its employment'. Racket makers and ball makers were much in demand.

THE HIGH BORNE PRINCE IAMES DVKE OF YORKE
borne October the 14. 1633.

It is well known that in his youth Henry VIII was a keen tennis player. He built a tennis court at Hampton Court Palace in 1530 that is still in use today—the oldest active tennis court in the world (for court dimensions see opposite page). Henry was following a custom long established among the royal houses of Europe. Charles X of France, a keen tennis player, had died in 1316 after catching a chill following a strenuous game of *Jeu de Paume*.

Shakespeare portrays the Dauphin, in answer to Henry V's claim to French territory in 1414, sending him a present of tennis balls. Responding to the taunt that he was more suited to playing games than fighting battles, Henry replies:

When we have matched our rackets to these balls,
We will, in France, by God's grace, play a set
Shall strike his father's crown into the hazard.

Henry was as good as his word. Victories over the French at Harfleur and Agincourt in 1415 were the prelude to his eventual recognition as the heir and Regent of France at the Treaty of Troyes in 1420.

Although Real Tennis courts were all slightly different in size they were roughly 110 feet long, 40 feet wide and 30 feet high with a net across the centre that was 5 feet high at its ends, falling to 3 feet in the centre. There was a flagstone floor and a narrow roof, the penthouse, on three sides of the court above galleries into which the ball could be driven to end a point. There was a serving end and a receiving end. The scoring system, based on 15, 30, 40 and game, included setting 'chases' (a second bounce as close as possible to the server's end wall), judged against lines painted across the floor of the court and recorded by a 'marker' who also kept the score. The rules are now laid down by the Tennis & Rackets Association, but have changed little since they were first formally introduced in 1599 at the same time as the standard court.

LIFE IN IMPERIAL BRITAIN

Lawn Tennis emerged in the middle of the nineteenth century, when Great Britain was a wealthy nation brimming with confidence. In an age when income tax was low, wealthy landowners and the new captains of industry produced by the Industrial Revolution enjoyed enviable lifestyles, living in large properties both in town and country. Servants catered to their every need. At weekends they were kept busy giving house parties in their country houses, where Croquet was a favourite pastime on summer afternoons.

Croquet required a flat and manicured lawn so that the large heavy balls could be struck accurately with a wooden mallet towards metal hoops hammered into the grass. Croquet had evolved from the French game *Paille Maille* (Pall Mall in England) and a similar game brought to England from Ireland. The first rules were registered in 1856 but were not widely published. Nevertheless, unstructured games of Croquet enjoyed great popularity in the 1850s and 1860s at house parties and on back lawns of family homes. When Walter Whitmore, a founder member of the All England Croquet Club, published a new set of rules in *The Field* in 1866, many casual players complained that the game was too scientific and lost interest. Young men and women were looking for a game that was more athletic and challenging.

LAWN TENNIS APPEARS

The man who answered their needs was Walter Clopton Wingfield. A captain in the 1st Dragoon Guards, Wingfield had retired in 1861 while still under the age of 30 and with no fixed idea of how to spend his time. The

family home, Rhysnant Hall, was in Llandysilio, Montgomeryshire, and he soon joined the Montgomeryshire Yeomanry Cavalry, remaining with them until he retired as a Major in 1873.

In 1870 Wingfield (right) was appointed to the Honourable Corps of

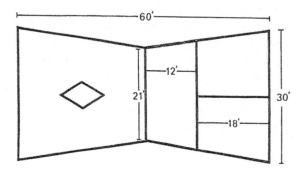

Gentlemen at Arms, the Queen's personal bodyguard. Thus Wingfield was well connected socially, and on his visits to the house parties of his wealthy friends towards the end of the 1860s he noticed that Croquet was losing its appeal. Seeing the opportunity for commercial success, in the spring of 1873 Wingfield, now living in London, put his mind to the invention of a new game, one that would be easily understood and easily played by men and women.

The result of his experiments was 'Sphairistike' (a Greek word loosely meaning skill with a ball), a simple game with only six rules. It could be played by two or four people on an hour-glass-shaped court (above), divided in half by a net. There were triangular pieces of side netting running from the net about one-third

of the way towards the baseline on both sides of the court. Rackets, similar to those used in Real Tennis but lighter and with a slightly larger head, would be used to hit a hollow India-rubber ball back and forth across the net. The serve was delivered from a diamond-shaped box at one end only. The receiver's end had a service line drawn roughly across the centre, and the area beyond was divided by another line into two equal portions. The serve had to bounce beyond the service line and in the diagonal service square. Curiously, Wingfield adopted the Rackets system of scoring, rather than tennis scoring. Games were of 15 aces (points), and the player who was hand-out could choose whether to set to 5 when the score reached 13-all, or to 3 at 14-all.

Wingfield obtained rackets from Jefferies and Mallings, a Woolwich firm. The balls came from Germany, and the posts and netting from local suppliers. He was soon ready to test the product. It was an immediate success and was popular with ladies as well as gentlemen. The days of Croquet were numbered.

It may have been at a demonstration of the game by 'a Captain of Artillery called Major Wingfield' in the garden of Lord Lansdowne's house in Berkeley Square that Arthur Balfour, the future prime minister, had suggested to Wingfield that Lawn Tennis would be a better name for his invention than Sphairistike, a word that no one understood. Balfour was right: Lawn Tennis was exactly the right name.

Wingfield immediately saw the need to protect his idea. Accordingly, early in 1874, he applied for

WOODCUT ADVERTISEMENT OF 1875 FOR A TENNIS OUTFIT
See letter: Early Lawn Tennis

a patent for the invention of 'A new and improved portable court for playing the ancient game of Tennis'. Note that Wingfield was not claiming to have invented Lawn Tennis. He had invented the portable court on which it would be played and had specified the rules that would apply. In Clause 15 of the patent application he leaves no doubt about his intentions:

> The object and intention of this Invention consists in constructing a portable court by means of which the ancient game of tennis is much simplified, can be played in the open air, and dispenses with the necessity of having special courts erected for that purpose.

17

On 25 February, just two days after receiving his patent, Wingfield printed his eight-page booklet of the game, which he must have been working on for months. Altogether there would be five editions printed between 1874 and 1876. On the first page, the following words appear: 'The Major's Game of Lawn Tennis, dedicated to the party assembled at Nantclwyd in December 1873 by W. C. W.'.

The party mentioned was a house-warming for Major Naylor-Leyland and his wife in their new home at Nantclwyd in North Wales, not a special gathering to observe the new game. It was a grand affair with some 200 guests invited, too many to be accommodated at Nantclwyd Hall. Many stayed at nearby Ruthin Castle, at other manor houses, and at local hotels. The party, lasting several days, included two plays in Ruthin Castle and a 'Grand Fancy Ball'. The experience made a lasting impression: all five editions of Wingfield's booklet were dedicated to the party assembled at Nantclwyd (see page 44).

As soon as he returned to London, Wingfield was quick to see that copies of the booklet, which included the Rules, were published in *The Field*, the *Court Journal* and the *Army and Navy Gazette,* as well as in other leading general and sporting journals. It was essential to inform the public of his new product if it was to sell in large numbers. Oddly, the width of the net was not mentioned in the Rules, although it was in the patent application. In a letter to *The Field* on 11 April 1874, responding to a reader's enquiry, Wingfield rectified the omission. The net was to be 21 feet wide and 4 feet 8 inches high.

COMPETING VERSIONS

Although no one can safely be credited with 'inventing' Lawn Tennis, we do know that Wingfield was not the first to experiment. Articles and letters in *The Field* suggest that several individuals had been playing a game with rackets and a rubber ball as early as the mid-1850s, although there is no concrete evidence. Two who could prove in 1872 that they had for some time been playing a game that is recognizable

as a forerunner of modern Lawn Tennis were Harry Gem (left) and Augurio Perera.

Gem, a solicitor, was a well-known personality in Birmingham who followed his father as clerk to the Birmingham magistrates.

Besides being a founder member of the city's Union Club he wrote humorous articles for local papers and magazines, and took part in amateur dramatics. As a young man Gem was a keen sportsman: he founded a cricket club in a Birmingham suburb in his early twenties and also played for Moseley Cricket Club. In his early forties Gem won a famous bet by running the twenty-one miles from Birmingham to Warwick in under three-and-a-half hours, wearing full morning dress, 'so as not to excite observation', he said!

Perera, a Spanish trader, had come to live in Birmingham in 1839. Over the next thirty years he built up a profitable business importing Spanish merchandise. Little is known about him, save his experiments with Gem on the croquet lawn behind Perera's house, Fairlight, in Ampton Road, Edgbaston.

Perera and Gem were both members of Birmingham's Bath Street Racquet Club, which Gem had founded in 1859 on the site of the old Racquet Court Tavern. Perera was the first to suggest to Gem that Rackets could easily be adapted as an outdoor game for the enjoyment of both men and women. At Fairlight they laid out an oblong court with a net, and hit a rubber ball to and fro with a larger-headed version of the racket they used in Rackets, strung with sheep gut. There is no record of any rules for this new

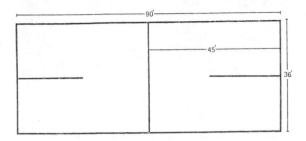

pastime, which they called 'Pelota' after the game popular in the Basque country.

In 1872 both Gem and Perera, now in their fifties, moved to Leamington Spa. Together with two young doctors, both in their twenties, they founded the Leamington Club that summer in the grounds of the Manor House Hotel, opposite Perera's new home in Avenue Road. So it was that Gem, Perera, Dr Frederic Haynes, and Dr Arthur Wellesley Tomkins became founder members of the first Lawn Tennis club in the world. It was renamed the Leamington Lawn Tennis Club in 1874 and each summer thereafter a tournament was held for the members. In November 1874 Harry Gem of Leamington wrote to *The Field* and sent a plan of his court. It was longer than the other courts and half as long again as the original Sphairistike court (above).

A first copy of the Rules, printed in 1874, following Wingfield's publication of his booklet in February,

was titled: *Lawn Tennis or Pelota—Rules of the Game as Played by the Leamington Club*. It is the only known copy of the original rule book to have survived. It was presented to the City of Birmingham by Harry Gem's widow soon after his death in November 1881. This was obviously Gem's own copy because he has made amendments, including the change of 'Rules' to 'Laws', all initialled in his own hand, in preparation for a reprint. It includes an illustration of the court by Harry Gem himself (above). It now resides in the Archives and Heritage Services section of Birmingham's Central Library. There are fifteen rules, nine more than in Wingfield's Sphairistike. The game, using Rackets scoring, could be played by two players (a single), three players (a unicorn) or four players (a double). The rectangular court was 90 feet long by 36 feet wide. The net was 4 feet high.

In the title of the second set of Rules, published on 1 January 1875, the 'Rules' changed to 'Laws'. However, in most respects the Rules themselves were unchanged.

It was his commercial expertise that set Wingfield apart from Harry Gem and others such as John Hale, who had also hastily published his version of the new game once Wingfield's booklet had appeared. Hale was a well-known cricketer. His Germains Lawn Tennis, named after his house in Chesham, Buckinghamshire, was announced in *The Field* of 24 October 1874. This version had a rectangular court (60 feet by 30 feet for singles, 72 feet by 30 feet for doubles) and a net 4 feet 6 inches in height that was, like Wingfield's, 21 feet wide. This was probably to allow those who had purchased a set of Sphairistike to play Germains Lawn Tennis, though

it meant there was a gap of 4 feet 6 inches down each wing, which seems curious. Note that these rules were published eight months after Wingfield's booklet had appeared.

The scoring system is the fifteen aces (points) of Rackets. The server, using 'a small tennis racket' delivers the ball from small boxes on the baseline, either side of the centre line, across the net and into a service square beyond the service line. There were eighteen rules altogether, with some more mysterious than others.

Germains Lawn Tennis, like Wingfield's Sphairistike, was sold in boxes at five guineas per set. Whether because of the complicated rules or lack of publicity, Germains Lawn Tennis had a short life. However, both the Germains rules and the Leamington rules included a rectangular court, and it was that shape which would ultimately be adopted by the All England Croquet and Lawn Tennis Club for their first tournament in 1877. It has survived to this day.

Wingfield's commercial success was considerable, yet he could not afford to admit it, using his initials instead of his full name in the booklet and in his early letters to *The Field*. As a gentleman, Wingfield could not be seen to be entering into trade. However, his friends would understand if he dealt with sales at arm's length and would be ready to congratulate him if the venture proved to be a success.

From the start he had appointed as his agent French & Co., a supplier of cricket equipment whose premises were three blocks away from his home at 112 Belgrave Road. They supplied his small and large boxes of 'Sphairistike or Lawn Tennis', which were priced at five guineas and £10 respectively. Inside each box was the same booklet, carrying the Rules that he advertised widely in magazines and periodicals, the back page of which carried the following announcement:

The game is in a painted Box, 36 x 12 x 6 in., and contains Poles, Pegs, and Netting for forming the Court, 4 Tennis Bats, by Jefferies and Mallings, a Bag of Balls, a Mallet and Brush and Book of the Game. It can only be obtained from the Inventor's agents, Messrs. French and Co., 46, Churton Street, London, S.W. Price five guineas.

We know from the day book of sales kept by French and Co. that in the four weeks from 6 July to 1 August 1874 they sold 353 large and small sets of Sphairistike, plus many separate rackets, balls, presses, and books of the game, several of them to overseas customers. Two retailers, Mr Cremer of Bond Street and Mr Buchanan of Piccadilly, were buying six, nine, or even twelve sets at a time.

Wingfield, ever the publicist, published a list of those to whom sets had been sold. It looks like a series of pages from *Burke's Peerage*. Headed by the Prince of Wales, there are ten members of European royal

1874. Monday July 6

The Countess Waldegrave
Strawberry Hill
Twickenham
+ Large Set Tennis 10 10 0
Paid W.B.

The Lady Hamilton
38 Upper Brook Street
Grosvenor Square
+ Berkhamsted House G.W. Berkhamsted
+ Set Tennis 5 5 -

The Lord Cawder
74 South Audley Street
+ Set Tennis 5 5 -
Paid W.B.

The Earl of Galloway

1874 Monday July 6

Lt Colonel F Maitland Wilson
40 Upper Brook Street
+ Large Set 10 10 -

Mr Lionel Ashley
23 Portman Square
+ Set Tennis 5 5 0
+ 2 Bats 20/- Balls 7/6 1 12 6
+ 2 Presses 1 10 -
Paid W.B. 8 7 6

The Hon W H B Portman M.P.
By Cash 6.5.0.4.

Lord Ashburton
By Cash 10.10.0 Tennis

families, seven dukes, sixteen marquises and one marchioness, the governor-general of Canada, fifty-four earls, twelve countesses, ten viscounts, forty-one lords, forty-four ladies, forty-five honourables, five MPs—including the speaker—and fifty-five knights of the realm. The impressive list ends with the British embassies in Calcutta, Constantinople, St Petersburg, and Rome plus the four clubs: Lord's, Hurlingham, Princes, and Lillie Bridge. Sets also went to the Life Guards, Royal Horse Guards and numerous regiments, also to Eton, Oxford, Cambridge, and various other colleges and schools. The game was fast becoming an international success; sets started to arrive in America in the summer of 1874. It was now safe for Wingfield to start signing his letters to *The Field* with his full name.

Yet individuals were playing by their own rules. Frequent letters to *The Field* called for change. Some wanted a rectangular court, others a wider and lower net. After Hale had published his Rules in *The Field* on 21 November 1874, Wingfield fought a strong rearguard action. One week later, on 28 November, he altered his 'perfect court' from 60 feet to 84 feet in length and from 30 feet

LAWN TENNIS

W. BADDELEY

to 39 feet at the baseline (see page 58). The two ends of the court were now identical and the serve was to be delivered from the baseline at either end, though ladies could stand on the service line. He reduced the height of the net to 4 feet 4 inches in the centre. The balls, he said, should be hollow, 2½ inches in diameter and 1⅓ ounces in weight. The bat should be of tennis shape, 27 inches long and weighing 12 ounces.

Clearly, someone needed to take the lead in seeking general agreement about how to go forward. At the suggestion of J. M. Heathcote, a prominent Real Tennis player and a member of the Marylebone Cricket Club (MCC), his club took a hand. Heathcote's proposal for a meeting of all interested parties at Lord's, where various versions of Lawn Tennis could be demonstrated and the rules discussed, was supported by Henry Jones, a founder member of the All England Croquet Club, who wrote under the pen name 'Cavendish' in *The Field*. Besides being the governing body of cricket, recently the Marylebone club had revised the rules of Real Tennis, which was keenly played at Lord's. These rules were accepted throughout the country.

A gathering took place on Wednesday 8 March 1875 at Lord's to discuss the merits of the competing versions of Lawn Tennis. Wingfield and Hale

29

demonstrated their versions of the game, but there is no record of Gem having attended. Following an open discussion, it was agreed that the Tennis Committee of the MCC should issue a new set of Rules for Lawn Tennis. These duly appeared on 24 May 1875 (see page 53).

Although Wingfield's hour-glass court was retained—to the dismay of Hale and Gem—the service now had to land in a service court between the net and the service line instead of beyond it as before. This fundamental change would launch the game in a new direction (for plan of court and dimensions see pages 52 and 53). The height of the net was 5 feet at the posts and 4 feet in the centre. The Rackets form of scoring was retained but with 'deuce and advantage' at 14-all. The ball dimensions were agreed at 2¼ inches in diameter and 1½ ounces in weight and they should be covered with cloth 'in fine weather only'. A note attached to the new rules stated that the court dimensions were those that applied to the court at Lord's.

Forthwith Wingfield agreed to the new rules and dropped his own. It was also in 1875 that the All England Croquet Club, at the urging of Henry Jones, introduced Lawn Tennis for the enjoyment of members at their ground off Worple Road, Wimbledon.

In April one croquet lawn was given over to the new sport. It quickly attracted a dozen new members. In 1876 a flood of new tennis members led to a third of the ground being given over to Lawn Tennis.

Despite the improvements in the new rules, there was still dissatisfaction, especially at Prince's Club, where they went on playing with a rectangular court, as did many other correspondents to *The Field*. There was also a call for the net to be lowered, the service line to be brought nearer the net, and for Tennis scoring to replace Rackets scoring. The MCC were asked to intervene but declined, and Wingfield, having agreed to allow the MCC rules to prevail, was silent.

By 1877 Lawn Tennis had become so popular at The All England Croquet Club that in April the name was changed to the All England Croquet and Lawn Tennis Club. On 2 June, at the suggestion of the club's secretary, John H. Walsh, the committee decided to hold a tournament. This would, they hoped, raise sufficient funds to repair the broken pony roller that was essential to the maintenance of the lawns. Walsh was also the editor of *The Field*, in whose offices the All England Croquet Club had been founded in 1868. In August 1872 he had originally donated the pony roller to the club in return for the election of his daughter to membership. Now that his committee had decided

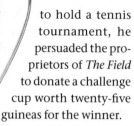

to hold a tennis tournament, he persuaded the proprietors of *The Field* to donate a challenge cup worth twenty-five guineas for the winner.

A sub-committee of three—Charles Gilbert Heathcote, Julian Marshall, and Henry Jones—was established to decide what rules should apply. They had to move fast so that public notice could be given and entry forms printed. Four days later the Championship Rules appeared in *The Field*. Mindful of all the public debate, but anxious not to offend the MCC by altering their rules too drastically, the club diplomatically issued a provisional set of rules just for the championship. They stipulated a rectangular court (see page 59 for dimensions). A centre line from net to baseline provided left and right courts. The net was still 5 feet high at the posts (which were placed 1 yard outside the sidelines), but was lowered to 3 feet 3 inches in the centre. The balls would be 2½ to 2⅝ inches in diameter and 1¾ ounces in weight, and Tennis scoring would be adopted. Service would be delivered from the baseline into the opposing diagonal service court, and the server would have two chances to make a good serve on every point. Players would change ends between sets. Not until 1898 did the Rules require a change of ends after every odd game.

That first championship was an outstanding success. Spencer Gore, an old Harrovian who had excelled at Rackets and Squash-Ball, a game peculiar to Harrow at the time, became the first champion.

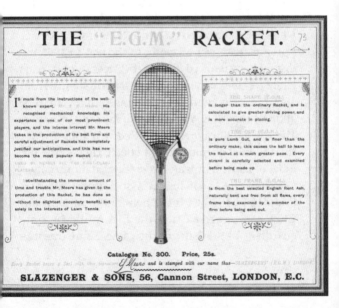

Some 200 spectators attended his final against William Marshall, and the profit from the meeting was £10, ample to pay for the repair of the roller.

The following May the MCC approached the All England Club and suggested that together they should issue a joint set of rules. The committee, which met to agree the terms, issued 'The Laws of Lawn Tennis as Adopted by the M.C.C. and the A.E.C. & L.T.C.' in May 1878. In the next few years the height of the net was reduced three times. In 1878 it came down to 4 feet 9 inches at the post and 3 feet in the centre. Two years later it fell to 4 feet at the posts and finally, in 1882, it was reduced to 3 feet 6 inches at the posts, where it has remained ever since. Similarly, the service line was twice moved closer to the net. In 1878 the distance was reduced from 26 to 22 feet and two years later to 21 feet, a measurement that still stands. From 1879 the MCC, while remaining as joint rule makers, allowed the All England Club to take the initiative. The few modifications introduced at Wimbledon for their annual championships effectively became the Rules of Lawn Tennis and were adopted universally.

When the Lawn Tennis Association (LTA) was founded in 1888 with the help of the All England Club, it was agreed that the LTA would become guardians of the Rules of the game. Some overseas

Garrison Lawn Tennis Club.

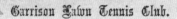

Annual ∴ Tournament,

1894,

ABBEY GARDENS, COLCHESTER,

MONDAY & TUESDAY, AUGUST 6TH & 7TH, 1894.

PLAY COMMENCES EACH DAY AT 2 P.M.

The Tournament will be played under the Rules of the A.E.L.T. Club. The decision of the Committee in all disputed points to be final. The best of three sets to decide each tie. No Vantage Games except in finals.

The order of play will be duly posted on notice board. Competitors absent when called on to play render themselves liable to be disqualified.

Tournament Committee.

Lt. Colonel HOUISON-CRAUFURD, D.A.A.G.

Major CHAYTOR, 2nd Northamptonshire Regt.

Surgeon Major JOHNSTON, A.M.S.

LEONARD DITMAS, Capt.,

Hon. Secretary.

PRICE—TWOPENCE.

Lingard, Printer, Colchester.

associations introduced special conditions for their own championships. In the United States, for example, the ladies' singles was played over five sets in 1891 and 1892, and again from 1894 to 1901. However, the game was played everywhere under the Rules of Lawn Tennis as established by the LTA. In 1913 the International Lawn Tennis Federation was created, but not until January 1924 did the new body (which became the International Tennis Federation (ITF) in 1977) take on this role. Today any modifications to the Rules are approved at the Annual General Meetings of the ITF's 205 member nations, and come into effect the following January. At present there are thirty Rules and seven Appendices that amplify various points within them.

Over the years the foot-fault rule has been modified three times. In 1874 the server was required to have his front foot on the baseline and his rear foot on the ground until the ball had been struck. From January 1903 the server was allowed to let his rear foot leave the ground, provided it did not cross the baseline before he struck the ball. From January 1955 swinging of the back foot across the baseline was allowed, but the front foot still had to remain in contact with the ground. However, with more and more players charging the net behind their serves, it was impossible for chair umpires operating without linesmen to decide if the server's foot had left the ground before he had struck the ball. Accordingly, in 1959 jumping was allowed. Today the rule is simple: a server must stand between the centre of the baseline and the singles sideline, must not alter position by walking or running, and must not touch the baseline or any part of the court beyond it until the ball has been struck.

The scoring system at Wimbledon was also modified. Until 1884, the year when the ladies' singles and men's doubles events were introduced, the first player to win six games won the set, as in Real Tennis. Accordingly, many matches included 6–5 sets. In 1884 advantage sets were introduced, although the Rules of Tennis still allowed tournaments to adopt 6–5 sets until 1 January 1913, when advantage sets became compulsory. From six games all the set continued until one player broke the other's serve to lead by two games. Thus, in theory a set could continue indefinitely and many were the matches when a set ended at 12–10, 15–13 or 18–16.

One of the most dramatic matches ever played at Wimbledon was in 1969, the second year of open tennis, when the most important tournaments first allowed professional players as well as amateurs to enter. It was between two Americans, Pancho Gonzales, the former king of the professionals, then aged 41, and Charlie Passarell, a US Davis Cup player, aged 25. Because of fading light the battle spanned two days and lasted five hours and twelve minutes to become Wimbledon's longest match at that stage. Eventually, after saving seven match points, the weary old lion won the battle of wills 22–24, 1–6, 16–14, 6–3, 11–9. The 112 games played remain a record.

With an increase in the number of indoor professional tournaments played on one or two courts, the tie-break became part of the game. However, the tie-break is included in the Rules of Tennis only as an option that can be adopted by tournaments, provided they give advance warning to competitors.

There have been several versions of the tie-break. At the US Open in 1970 the nine-point sudden-death tie-break was introduced at six games all. The brainchild of the eccentric American millionaire Jimmy Van Alen who founded the International Tennis Hall of Fame in Newport, Rhode Island, sudden death involved a one-point decider at 4–4 with the umpire raising a red flag to signify sudden death. The receiver could decide which court he would receive from. This was high drama. The players hated it; the fans loved it. In the present tie-break the first player to reach seven points with at least a two-point advantage wins the set. From six points all, play continues until one player has a two-point advantage.

The tie-break was introduced at Wimbledon in 1971 when the score reached eight games all (altered to six games all from 1979) in every set except the fifth in men's matches and the third in women's matches. That system continues today and is also used at the Grand Slams in Australia and France. However, at the US Open all sets still end in a tie-break at six games all. All tournaments on the men's and women's professional tours include tie-breaks in all sets for singles matches.

It was not until 1979 that rackets were mentioned in the Rules of Tennis. That is because over the years a wooden racket had evolved to an optimum length of 27 inches and a weight of between 12 ounces and 16 ounces due to human physiology. Any heavier and it would be too difficult to wield; any lighter and it would warp. Equally, the head size of approximately 78 square inches was determined by the ability of the frame to take high tensions of stringing without collapsing.

In 1965 René Lacoste, one of the four French 'Musketeers', patented a small-headed steel racket, which was marketed in the US as the Wilson T2000. It was the racket used with great success by Jimmy Connors throughout his career. Thus began a flood of new steel, aluminium, and fibreglass rackets in the late 1960s and early 1970s that became popular both with club players and the professionals because they were lighter and easier to wield than wooden rackets. For a while the oversize Prince racket, made of graphite and with a head size of 110 square inches, became the racket of choice for many tournament players.

By the 1970s experiments with the stringing system were also appearing. One had two sets of strings strung to a low tension, one each side of the head, and heavy knotted in the centre. In 1977 at the US Open an American player called Michael Fishbach, ranked below 200 in the world, used a racket invented by Werner Fischer, an amateur player from Bavaria. In the centre of the strings was an area about 6 inches square where the strings were knotted. These 'spaghetti rackets' allowed tremendous topspin to be imparted to the ball so that incredible cross-court angles were possible. Sensationally Fishbach reached the third round. His fizzing topspin had been too much for the former US Junior champion Billy Martin and the no. 16 seed Stan Smith, the 1972 Wimbledon champion.

In September that year Christophe Roger-Vasselin, a moderate French player, used a spaghetti racket at the Coupe Porée in Paris and unexpectedly reached the final, where he lost to the Argentine left-hander, Guillermo Vilas. In the Aix en Provence final the following week Vilas, attempting to extend his record streak of fifty-three consecutive winning matches on clay, faced his old foe, Ilie Nastase. The wily Romanian decided to use one of the new spaghetti rackets for the match. Vilas was furious. After losing the first two sets 6–1, 7–5 he stormed off the court and refused to finish the match.

The ITF was quick to react. On 3 October the spaghetti racket was temporarily banned. At their 1978 AGM the ITF introduced a new rule that came into effect the following January. Rule 4 declared that only single stringing was legal. A note added to the new rule stated: 'The spirit of this rule is to prevent undue spin on the ball that would result in a change in the nature of the game.' Thereafter several additions describing the maximum length and width of the frame were introduced. Under the present rules a racket cannot exceed 29 inches in length or 12½ inches in width. The stringing system cannot be more than 15½ inches long or 11½ inches wide.

Today, international tennis has become a major multimillion-dollar industry. It is the most widely played individual ball game in the world. At the professional level its superstars are household names, instantly recognized even by their first names. Roger and Rafa, Pete and Boris, André and Bjorn, Martina, Steffi, Monica, Venus, and Serena—all have entered the realm of sporting folklore.

Looking back, it is remarkable that during the productive nineteenth century the British, searching for new ways of filling their leisure time with athletic pursuits, would codify and publish rules for Football, Rugby Football, Croquet, Rackets, Badminton, Lawn

Tennis, Squash and Fives. Two other sports, Cricket and Golf, had emerged with rules a century earlier.

Though all of these sports and games could trace their origins to the dim and distant past, it was only when they had become properly structured and organized with an approved set of rules that they would spread around the world. Thanks to the far- reaching influence of the British Empire and the large number of overseas military bases, this was a rapid process. In no time, from Salisbury to Sydney, Delhi to Durban, Toronto to Trinidad, footballers, cricketers and tennis players were enjoying themselves in serious as well as social competition. Today, they still are.

FURTHER READING

Aberdare, Lord, *The J. T. Faber Book of Tennis and Rackets*, London, updated 2001.

Alexander, George, *Wingfield—Edwardian Gentleman*, Portsmouth, NH, 1986.

De Garsault, F. A., *Art du Paumier-Racquetier et de la Paume*, Paris, 1767.

Marshall, Julian, *Annals of Tennis*, London, 1878.

The Field Magazine, London, 1874, 1875.

Todd, Tom, *The Tennis Players*, Guernsey, 1979.

THE MAJOR'S GAME

OF

𝕷𝖆𝖜𝖓 𝕿𝖊𝖓𝖓𝖎𝖘,

DEDICATED TO

THE PARTY ASSEMBLED

AT

NANTCLWYD.

IN

DECEMBER, 1873.

BY

W. C. W.

LONDON:
HARRISON AND SONS, 59, PALL MALL.
[ENTERED AT STATIONERS' HALL.]

THE MAJOR'S GAME OF LAWN TENNIS

THE GAME OF TENNIS may be traced back to the days of the ancient Greeks, under the name of (σφαιριστικὴ). It was subsequently played by the Romans under the name of "Pila." It was the fashionable pastime of the nobles of France, during the reign of Charles V., and it was in vogue in England as early as Henry III., and is described by Gregory as "one of the most ancient games in Christendom." "Henry V.," "Henry VII.," and "Henry VIII." were all Tennis players, and it has only now died out owing to the difficulties of the game, and the expense of erecting courts. All these difficulties have been now surmounted by the inventor of "Lawn Tennis," which has all the interest of "Tennis," and has the advantage that it may be played in the open air in any weather by people of any age and of both sexes. In a hard frost the nets may be erected on the ice, and the players being equipped with skates, the Game assumes a new feature, and gives an opening for the exhibition of much grace and science.

Croquet, which of late years has monopolized the attention of the public, lacks the healthy and manly excitement of "Lawn Tennis." Moreover, this game

has the advantage that, while an adept at Tennis or Racquets would speedily become a really scientific player, the merest tyro can learn it in five minutes sufficiently well for all practical purposes.

ERECTION OF THE COURT

The space required for the erection of a perfect "Lawn Tennis" Court is 20 yards by 10. The ground need not even be turf; the only condition is, it must be level. On any ground where Croquet is played, a perfect "Lawn Tennis Court" could be put up in five minutes after the arrival of the box (containing the game).

Having selected a suitable piece of ground of the size mentioned above, four pegs, A, B, C, D, are placed as in the illustration. The distances at which these pegs are placed from each other to be as nearly as possible the same as given in the illustration.

The distances from A to B and from C to D are 10 yards, and A to C and from B to D are 20 yards, so each Court is 10 yards broad at the base, and 10 yards deep; the depth may, however, be increased if desirable.

The posts E and F will then be placed square across the centre, and the netting stretched betwixt them.

The two wings or side-nettings will then be secured to the posts E and F, by the loops and strings attached for the purpose, and the extremities drawn tight in the direction of the pegs A, B, C, D, forming thereby the side walls of the Court, and also the guy[1] rope to support the posts and centre netting.

The space (G) represents the In-Court, and the player who serves the ball must take his post in the crease H, which is in the centre.

The other space K forms the Out-Court, and must be divided by lines L, M, and N, O, drawn as marked in the plan.

The boundaries of the Court, and the service crease, which is one yard square, may be marked in white, for which purpose a brush will accompany the box, and a mixture of chalk or lime and water should be made in a bucket.

RULES

I.

This Game can be played by two or four players.

II.

The Game consists of 15 aces, and the out-side have the option of setting it, if they should happen to be 13 or 14 all, to either 3 to 5.

---

1 Guy ropes are also sent, they will be found round the box.

III.

The sides having been made, and the one to go in having been determined on, as in Racquets, they place themselves in court G, the first player standing in the service crease in the centre of the court, and serves, which he does by throwing up the ball with his left hand into the air, and while falling striking it with his bat and sending it over the net between E and F, first into one court and then into the other. The out-side stand one in the right, and the other in the left court of side K; if they fail to return the ball served to them during its first bound, or by a "volley," that is, hitting it before it has touched the ground, the in-side score an ace; but if they do return it, the ball is hit backwards and forwards over the net till one side fails to do so, or hits it out of Court.

IV.

The outer hand can never score an ace, he can merely put his opponent's hand out; the score can only be made by the side that is in.

V.

If the server does not hit the ball over the net between E and F, or sends it out of Court, or fails twice running to serve it into the proper Court, his hand is out.

VI.

With four players, the side that goes in has only one hand the first round.

This Game has been tested practically at several Country Houses during the past few months, and has been found so full of interest and so great a success, that it has been decided to bring it before the Public, being protected

by

HER MAJESTY'S ROYAL
LETTERS PATENT

USEFUL HINTS

Hit your ball gently, and look well before striking, so as to place it in the corner most remote from your adversary. A great deal of side can be imparted to the ball by the proper touch, which, together with a nice appreciation of strength, adds much to the delicacy and science.

RULES

OF

LAWN-TENNIS,

Adopted by the M.C.C. and the A.E.C. & L.T.C.
By PERMISSION, *verbatim.*

The Court is 27 feet in width, and 78 feet in length. It is divided across the middle by a net, the ends of which are attached to the tops of two posts, **A** and **A**, which stand 3 feet outside the Court on each side. The height of the net is 4¾ feet at the posts, and 3 feet at the centre. At each end of the Court, parallel with the net, and at a distance of 39 feet from it, are drawn the *Base-Lines*, **C D** and **E F**, the extremities of which are connected by the *Side-Lines*, **C E** and **D F**. Half-way between the Side-Lines, and parallel with them, is drawn the *Half-Court-Line*, **G H**, dividing the space on each side of the net into two equal parts, called the *Right* and *Left Courts*. On each side of the net, at a distance of 22 feet from it, and parallel with it, are drawn the *Service-Lines*, **X X** and **Y Y**.

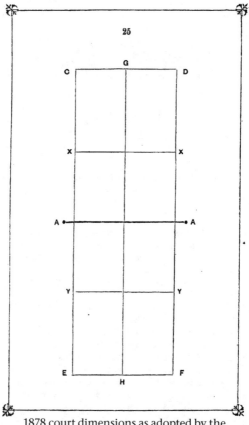

1878 court dimensions as adopted by the
MCC and the AEC & LTC

RULES OF LAWN-TENNIS,

Adopted by the M.C.C. and the A.E.C. & L.T.C.

By Permission, verbatim.

The Court is 27 feet in width, and 78 feet in length. It is divided across the middle by a net, the ends of which are attached to the tops of two posts, A and A, which stand 3 feet outside the Court on each side. The height of the net is 4¾ feet at the posts, and 3 feet at the centre. At each end of the Court, parallel with the net, and at a distance of 39 feet from it, are drawn the *Base-Lines*, C D and E F, the extremities of which are connected by the *Side-Lines*, C E and D F. Half-way between the Side-Lines, and parallel with them, is drawn the *Half-Court-Line*, G H, dividing the space on each side of the net into two equal parts, called the *Right* and *Left Courts*. On each side of the net, at a distance of 22 feet from it, and parallel with it, are drawn the *Service-Lines*, X X and Y Y.

In the three-handed and four-handed games the Court is 36 feet in width, and the height of the net at the posts 4 feet. Otherwise the Court is as above.

The balls shall be not less than 2½ inches, nor more than 2⅝ inches in diameter; and not less than 1¾ oz, nor more than 2 oz in weight.

~~~~~~~~~~~~~~~~~~~~~~~~

Laws of the Game

----

1. The choice of sides and the right of serving during the first game shall be decided by toss; provided that, if the winner of the toss choose the right to serve, the other player shall have the choice of sides, and *vice versa*. The players shall stand on opposite sides of the net; the player who first delivers the ball shall be called the *Server*, the other the *Striker-out*. At the end of the first game, the Striker-out shall become Server, and the Server shall become the Striker-out; and so on alternately in the subsequent games of the set.

2. The Server shall stand with one foot outside the Base-Line, and shall deliver the service from the Right and Left courts alternately, beginning from the Right. The ball served must drop within the Service-Line, Half-Court-Line, and Side-Line of the Court which is diagonally opposite to that from which it was served, or upon any such line.

3.   It is a *fault* ball if the ball served drop in the net, or beyond the Service-Line, or if it drop out of Court, or in the wrong Court. A fault may not be taken. After a fault, the Server shall serve again from the same Court from which he served that fault.

4.   The service may not be *volleyed*, i.e., taken before it touches the ground.

5.   The Server shall not serve until the Striker-out is ready. If the latter attempt to return the service, he shall be deemed to be ready. A good service delivered when the Striker-out is not ready annuls a previous fault.

6.   A ball is *returned*, or *in-play*, when it is played back, over the net, before it has touched the ground a second time.

7.   It is a good service or return, although the ball touch the net.

8.   The Server wins a stroke, if the Striker-out volley the service; or it he fail to return the service or the ball in-play; or if he return the service or ball in-play so that it drop outside any of the lines which bound his opponent's Court; or if he otherwise lose a stroke, as provided by Law 10.

9.   The Striker-out wins a stroke, if the Server serve two consecutive faults; or if he fail to return the ball

in-play; or if he return the ball in-play so that it drop outside any of the lines which bound his opponent's Court; or if he otherwise lose a stroke, as provided by Law 10.

10. Either player loses a stroke, if the ball in-play touch him or anything that he wears or carries, except his racket in the act of striking; or if he touch or strike the ball in-play with his racket more than once.

11. On either player winning his first stroke, the score is called 15 for that player; on either player winning his second stroke, the score is called 30 for that player; on either player winning his third stroke, the score is called 40 for that player; and the fourth stroke won by either player is scored game for that player; except as below:—

> If both players have won three strokes, the score is called deuce; and the next stroke won by either player is scored advantage for that player. If the same player win the next stroke, he wins the game; if he lose the next stroke, the score is again called deuce; and so on until either player win the two strokes immediately following the score of deuce, when the game is scored for that player.

12. The player who first wins six games wins a set; except as follows:—

If both the players win five games, the score is called games-all; and the next game won by either player is scored advantage-game for that player. If the same player win the next game, he wins the set; if he lose the next game, the score is again called games-all; and so on until either player win the two games immediately following the score of games-all, when he wins the set.

NOTE.—Players may agree not to play advantage-sets, but to decide the set by one game after arriving at the score of games-all.

13. The players shall change sides at the end of every set. When a series of sets is played, the player who was Server in the last game of one set shall be Striker-out in the first game of the next.

APPENDIX

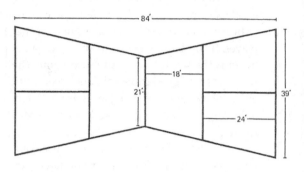

Wingfield's third court plan – November 1874

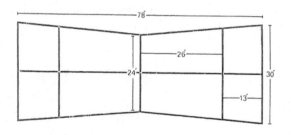

MCC-adopted court plan – May 1875

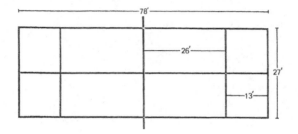

All England Club court plan – June 1877

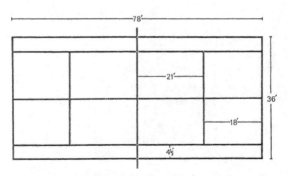

All England Club/MCC court plan for singles and
doubles – 1882